JUAN M. C. OLIVER

Shaped by
Worship

Liturgy and Formation

CHURCH
PUBLISHING
INCORPORATED

A little
book on
liturgy

Church Publishing
19 East 34th Street
New York, NY 10016

Cover design by Jennifer Kopec, 2Pug Design
Typeset by Denise Hoff

Library of Congress Cataloging-in-Publication Data

Names: Oliver, Juan M. C., author.
Title: Shaped by worship : liturgy and formation / Juan M.C. Oliver.
Description: New York, NY : Church Publishing, [2022] | Series: Little books on liturgy | Includes bibliographical references.
Identifiers: LCCN 2022020785 (print) | LCCN 2022020786 (ebook) | ISBN 9781640655904 (paperback) | ISBN 9781640655911 (ebook)
Subjects: LCSH: Liturgics. | Episcopal Church. | Spiritual formation--Episcopal Church.
Classification: LCC BX5940 .O45 2022 (print) | LCC BX5940 (ebook) | DDC 264--dc23/eng/20220608
LC record available at https://lccn.loc.gov/2022020785
LC ebook record available at https://lccn.loc.gov/2022020786

Contents

Preface

Just as liturgical formation is much more than an individual affair, this short book is the result of thirty years of interactions with a host of people who gradually opened my eyes to liturgical formation, what it is and what it is not. The list is too long to include here, but some people have been so important that they should be remembered and thanked.

Undergirding this book is the baptismal understanding of the church and its worship, masterfully informing every page in the Book of Common Prayer 1979, and the work of one of its main authors, my teacher and mentor, the Rev. Louis Weil.

As early as the 1980s, the late Robert Brooks and later, Michael Merriman, began the recovery and implementation of a process of baptismal formation, frequently called the catechumenate, in the Episcopal Church. This process included time set aside for reflection on the experience of Holy Baptism, what the early church called *mystagogy* or "leading into the mysteries." Soon after, the department of evangelism asked us to develop training seminars. These were extremely important as we explored ways and methods of not only preparing candidates for baptism, confirmation, reception, and other renewals of the baptismal covenant, but of continuing the conversation after the sacraments to open up their many meanings through reflection on what had been experienced.

My thanks go also to Michael Aune and the faculty of the Graduate Theological Union for insisting that liturgical studies had to include anthropological research in ritual studies.

More recently, Lisa Kimball's project at Virginia Theological Seminary, *Baptized for Life*, engaged me in fine-tuning reflection on the experience of worship. Her indomitable commitment to Christian formation made this excursion a pure joy.

All along, I adopted and adapted many of these insights at several congregations in the Bay Area, at the Mercer School of Theology, the General Theological Seminary, and most recently at St. Bede's in Santa Fe. My deep appreciation goes to all the stalwarts who put up with my attempts to practice what I describe in this book, by allowing the sacramental signs to speak fully and clearly, and in coming together to reflect upon our liturgical experience.

Finally, my deepest thanks to my patient and generous editor, Samuel Torvend, and to my husband, Johnny Lorenzo, who lovingly cared for me during an illness as I thought about these matters.

Santa Fe, New Mexico
Easter 2022

Introduction

When I was a Roman Catholic altar boy, growing up in Puerto Rico in the 1950s, the only time we talked about "formation" was in reference to seminaries. In Catholic seminaries, candidates for the priesthood were taught theology but were also *formed* as priests through a process of spiritual direction, self-examination, reflection, and the practice of Christian virtues.

Imagine my surprise when in the 1980s the Episcopal Church began to talk about the formation of *all* Episcopalians. Previously we had spoken of "Christian education," a term that implied the transferal of knowledge or information from one person to another. To speak of formation was something new and suggested that we were committed as a church to the development of the whole person as a Christian—not only one's mind and understanding, but also one's feelings, attitudes, and behaviors.

It was a pivotal moment. After centuries of assuming that the surrounding culture made Christians as if by osmosis, the church was beginning to accept that, as the North African theologian, Tertullian, wrote in the third century, "Christians are made, not born," and that without some

1

clarity about *how* this process might work, we were doomed to become utterly irrelevant or utterly secular. For Christendom, the Christian culture in which we lived, moved, and had our being, is now a thing of the past. People join the church today because they want to, with not much political or social status to gain. To put it bluntly: we cannot count on our culture to form people as Christians.

Thus "Christian formation" became a significant dimension of our common life, and today it is the name we give to the conscious development of the whole person—mind, body, and spirit—as a Christian, whether this formation takes place in the parish or the seminary, beginning before baptism, during childhood, and developing throughout our lives, for it is a never-ending process. Within the wider spectrum of formation, *liturgical* formation takes pride of place, if, as we claim, worship is at the core of who we are. Thus *formation in liturgy for our life of the world* is increasingly crucial, and it is important if not downright urgent to understand *what* it is—and what it is not—and *how* it works—or can fail to work.

So reflect for a minute on what role worship has played in your growth and development as a Christian. *How* has liturgy worked to form you? How have you been accompanied and nurtured in worship? How has your experience of worship responded to your needs and aspirations, informing how you live your life? Do we only *understand* concepts in worship, or is there more going on? These questions are the core of this little volume, intended to assist worshippers, lay and clergy alike, in developing a deeper understanding of the relationship between liturgy, formation, and mission in our daily lives, a relationship at the core of who we are as the People of God in Christ.

In what follows I first sketch a quick picture of what liturgy is and how it works as a form of human religious ritual, a time and place set apart to *do* something significant in the presence of God. What we do in liturgy, however, is much more than saying or singing words; we perform certain actions, physical actions that work as *signs*. These actions also involve people and objects, which in the process also become signs. These signs—actions, persons, and objects—become the ways or means through which God's grace is received by the worshipper: as signs, they must signify or mean, and it is precisely through meaning it that they effect God's grace on the worshipper. In this way, they *form us* with an attitude towards the world and a way of living in it. All this takes place through physical practice, and not only through thinking.

The second chapter explores the process by which our worship forms us and helps us to make meaning and purpose in life. I say "makes," for as we shall see, meaning is not something inert, lying "out there" or in a library, but something we do: a type of human action essential to our humanity. The meaning that we make in and through worship is first of all personal: for example, the meaning or significance *for you* of receiving communion. But communion, something we do together, also has a *shared* meaning: the significance of receiving communion with the whole Christian people traveling over two millennia across places and cultures. Both types of meaning—personal and communal—are involved in the liturgical experience.

We will then take a closer look at how the liturgy forms us in Christian faith and life. What is liturgical formation and how do we facilitate it, first of all in and through the liturgical action itself? For liturgical formation, as we shall see, is much more than sharing information *about* worship, but rather takes place primarily through participation in worship with full awareness of what is going on and what it might mean to us individually and as the Christian community. Beyond participation in worship, however, liturgical formation also involves our reflection upon our experience of it, individually and through conversation with each other, in dialogue with the treasure house of meanings that we have accumulated over centuries as a living tradition.

The final chapter examines the obstacles and challenges we often face when attempting to engage in liturgical formation in the parish today, and offers some pointers to guide liturgical formation of the whole congregation. We will consider how the actions of the liturgy can become opaque or shriveled over time and suggest that liturgical actions need to return to the full and complete use of signs. We then proceed to suggest ways in which we can recover intentional, scheduled reflection upon our experience of worship, both in small groups and through liturgical preaching. A brief summary of the chapter and some conclusions follow, ending with questions for discussion and a bibliography.

1 ■ How Does the Liturgy Work?

Liturgy is the Christian version of something essential to most human cultures: religious ritual, a practice so prevalent in the world's cultures that we should not allow the growing disinterest in Christian liturgy in the first world to blind us to how essential it is for the rest of humanity.

In this chapter, we explore liturgy first of all as a type of human ritual that shapes and forms us as Christians through practices in a time and place set apart—practices distinguished from everyday life in order to do something of importance related to God, ourselves, and the rest of creation. We will also see—and this might be a surprise if you think worship is a book—that the liturgy is much more than words. In worship, we carry out actions that work as *signs* through which God and God's grace are present to us and form us with an attitude toward the world and how we are called as Christians to live in it. This takes place not only through our understanding but also through our actions in worship and through our feelings as well. These actions, when they are working well as signs, inspire and animate our capacity to discover meaning in worship.

Liturgy as Ritual

Christian worship is a form of human ritual. We humans do rituals all over the place, for all sorts of reasons. From a scheduled football game to the family gathering at Thanksgiving, to school graduations and birthday parties, we set apart times and places to do something meaningful to us in a more or less structured way. These events, modest or very grand, are also patterned: they have norms, musts and must nots, even a history. They also identify us as part of a larger community, whether it be a team, network, family, neighborhood, or nation. Religious rituals do all this, of course, in relation to whatever the religion considers its ultimate or transcendent reality: for Christians, the God revealed in Jesus Christ. *Christian ritual or liturgy is thus an ensemble of actions at a place and time set apart, expressing and forming us into who we are as a community: the church, the People of God in Christ.*

Religious rituals have a way of presenting themselves as sacred, even authoritative, sanctioning different aspects of our personal and communal lives. Religious rituals crown queens, consecrate religious leaders, join couples in marriage, and deal properly with human remains. The authority and sacredness of religious ritual is framed and even constituted by its separation in time and place from everyday life. The chalice at the Eucharist, for example, is not sacred because of its design or costly metal, but because it is *employed* in a sacred action.

Of course we can find other experiences in life to be "sacred" apart from religious rituals. Rudolf Otto referred to these experiences as "numinous"—an experience of transcendence, whether a "higher power" or God—in nature, relationships, and throughout all our lives.[1] The numinous, or holy, is therefore not limited to liturgy, and can break into our lives to remind us that there is more to life than what is apparent.

At the core of religious ritual, however, is the "sacred" as a place and time set apart from daily life. Of course, a sacred place is actually the same as an ordinary place: what makes it "sacred" is the ritual *action* through which God is present, whether that be the consecration of a church or the circle formed by worshippers to celebrate the Eucharist at a picnic table in the woods. Liturgy as a religious ritual gives us a sacred "lens" through which we can view and experience all of life as sacred as well. Thus Christian liturgy reveals something we are not accustomed to living with on a daily basis: that *all reality is sacred* and is a manifestation of God's love. Christian liturgy can take us out of our self-absorbed focus and lead us to discover the presence of God in all things: in the waters of baptism and in a flowing river; in the Holy Eucharist and in the holiday dinner; in the Word of God and in the poem or love letter.

---

1 Rudolph Otto, *The Idea of the Holy* (Eastford, CT: Martino's Fine Books, 2010).

9

Ironically, the term "liturgy," from the Greek *leitourgia*, originally had no religious connotation. In the ancient Greek city-states, citizens (male landowners) had the obligation to do work (*orgē*) for the welfare of all the people (*laos*). They might build a road, construct a bridge, equip a company of soldiers, or finance a new play. This activity was termed *leitourgia*. So liturgy was, first and foremost, work done on behalf of the people and their well-being, "public works," if you will. Think of it this way: your taxes are used to help you and other citizens. Your taxes are a liturgy: work that benefits citizens.

When the Hebrew Bible was translated into Greek, the Hebrew word *avodah* ("service to God in the temple") was translated as *leitourgia* to God. And so "liturgy" came to mean both a service to the people and a service to God. The term, therefore, does not properly refer *only* to a Christian worship service, but also to all Christian work in service to others—especially the poor, the sick, and the creation itself. In this sense, the corner soup kitchen is also a form of liturgy.

Sacrament and Mystery

Let us consider another common term: many of our liturgies involve a "sacrament." The term does not simply mean "something very sacred." Originally, it referred to a soldier's sacred (*sacra*) oath (*mentum*) of fidelity to the emperor or to his commander. In the third century, Tertullian wrote that a Christian soldier could not take a *sacramentum* of loyalty because in baptism he had already sworn allegiance to Jesus Christ. This is how the term "sacrament" entered the vocabulary of Western Christianity. At first it referred to baptism and later to other rituals of significance in the Christian community. In its original meaning, a sacrament is a pledge, both *God's* pledge of God's grace for us, and *our* pledge to God given in trusting faith. Moreover, Christian sacraments are, according to the ancient definition first crafted by Augustine and repeated in our Catechism, "outward and visible *signs* of inward and spiritual grace" (Book of Common Prayer 857). They are signs, and in what follows we will therefore pay special attention to the sacramental signs and what they mean.

Since the fourth century, the Eastern Orthodox churches have used the term *mysterion* or "mystery" to refer to what Westerners call sacraments. Before that, in the New Testament, *mysterion* did not refer to worship, but to God's hidden plan for all creation. The term *mysterion,* however, long in use before Christ, was used to refer to Mediterranean mystery religions, their stories and ritual. In these religions, people preparing for initiation experienced a process of instruction and conversion that involved an "initiation." These terms—mystery and initiation—were adapted by early Christians to describe the process of being incorporated into the wounded and risen body of Christ through baptism, anointing, and Eucharist: one single ritual of

11

incorporation. In the same way, the term "illumination," not coined by Christians, was used to describe what happens in Holy Baptism as the newly baptized is enlightened by the Spirit.

In Christianity, however, the term *mystery* does not mean something unknown, like the murderer in a mystery novel. When we refer to the liturgy as a mystery, we are not saying that the liturgy is incomprehensible or mystifying. Rather, we are saying that the liturgy and the sacrament celebrated in the liturgy are a *sign that leads us into something beyond itself.* In a very real sense, sacraments reveal or point us to something else. If they do not point, they are not working as signs. Here's an example: if I must first explain to a friend what I am doing by giving the friend a hug, the hug is not working on its own as a sign of friendship. An explanation is better than nothing, but when the sign— the action—is experienced as a transparent expression of what it means, the meaning comes through without need for any explanation.

Liturgy, therefore, is not a mystery in the sense of something secret or hidden, because, to quote the author of Colossians, "the mystery that has been hidden (God's secret plan) throughout the ages and generations … has now been *revealed* …" (Col. 1:26; also Eph. 3:9). This revelation of God's hidden, loving plan for all creation was revealed in the person of Jesus of Nazareth, his announcement of the impending arrival of God's reign (kingdom) here on earth, his healings and miracles, his declaring forgiveness freely, without condition, and his confronting the religious charlatans ("hypocrites") of his day—all of which led him to the cross, where he triumphed over the powers of evil and death that corrupt and destroy God's creatures.

This revelation of God's secret plan does, however, involve some *real* mysteries to which our liturgical actions point, but about which we do *not* keep quiet: mysteries such as God and God becoming flesh, as well as the unending life of Christ, in whom we are incorporated through baptism as limbs of his wounded and risen Body, and the presence of God's coming reign of truth, justice, peace, and love already among us, even though it has not yet fully arrived.

Real Mysteries

The great Jesuit theologian Karl Rahner wrote that God is a mystery in the sense that the more we approach God the more there is to approach.[2] Like the horizon, ever unfolding as we try to reach it, God is infinite and always more than we can comprehend. This is the first *real* mystery involved in worship: No matter how much we try to domesticate God, God is *always* more than we can think or imagine. Thus the liturgy reveals aspects of the mystery

---

2 Karl Rahner, "The Concept of Mystery in Catholic Theology," *Theological Investigations*, vol. IV (New York: Herder and Herder, 1973).

that is God through the sign actions and in a very real sense, draws our attention to God's presence.

Our tradition also includes another mystery: God is three in one, "neither confounding the Persons, nor dividing the Substance" (Book of Common Prayer 864). This logical impossibility has been studied, debated, and fought over for centuries. And it still remains a mystery, part of the endless mystery that is God who is a community. Another real mystery is the enfleshment of God as a human being, for as God's action, we cannot comprehend it entirely. Another is the death and resurrection of Jesus Christ and his presence in his wounded and risen Body, the church, as first noted by St. Paul: "Now you are the body of Christ and individually members of it" (1 Cor. 12:27, but see also 10:16–17, 12:12, and 12:25–26; Gal. 3:27; Rom. 12:4–5, 6–8; Eph. 1:22, 2:19–22, 4:11–13; and Col. 1:18, 24; 3:15). The author of Ephesians could not contain himself: "This is a great mystery: I speak of Christ and his Church" (Eph. 5:32). The Church at worship *is* the body of the wounded and risen Christ. When you receive "the Body of Christ" in your hands, the phrase is not referring only to the bread, but to you and to the gathered church as well.

Finally, the presence of the promised reign or kingdom of God, already breaking through in the Church's liturgy although it has not yet fully arrived among us, is an unfathomable mystery as well. It is to mysteries such as these that the liturgical actions point. In the liturgy, therefore, mystery is neither mystification nor mysteriousness, but the deep realities revealed through an ensemble of signs, of actions, making them present for our contemplation, formation, and living out in daily life.

Signs

The liturgy, then, is an ensemble of *signs*. Our lives are full of them. Not only traffic signs, but also much richer, complex sign-actions, like sharing a meal or a hug. Signs are always expressions of something beyond themselves. They always have two parts: the *sign* (arms around a person, for example), and what is signified (friendship or love). In the history of liturgical theology we have tended to concentrate on the signified and made present —the Real Presence of Christ in the Eucharist, for example—and paid little attention to the sign: a gathered community sharing a meal. In liturgical formation we will try to keep both elements in balance: the sign and what it signifies, for it is in the relationship between sign and signified that the meaning of the sign dwells.

Some signs are designed to convey a single meaning. A red octagon with STOP on it directly conveys an order to stop your vehicle without any other possible interpretation. Other signs, however, convey more than one meaning. A birthday party, for example, means much more than, "you are older now." It also means "we love you, and we are happy you exist."

Moreover, our liturgical signs are not only the objects engaged in worship. In fact, in the liturgy it is the *actions* that are the main signs. In the Eucharist, for example, we gather, listen to God, share the meaning of God's Word, pray for the needs of the world and the church, present offerings, give thanks to God, share food and drink, and are sent into the world again. These are the building blocks or *elemental signs* of our eucharistic worship. They involve, of course, persons who are also signs and objects—all of them sacred signs since they are involved in a sacred action.

All liturgy is therefore *embodied*. For the most part it does not consist only of ideas expressed verbally, for ninety-five percent of human communication is non-verbal. It is not mostly a collection of words, but a series of actions by bodies gathered at a given time, place, and in a specific culture. We do liturgy, and it cannot be fully understood without doing it, just like one cannot understand swimming without getting wet. A personal anecdote makes the point:

Many years ago, as I prepared to leave San Francisco for the East Coast, I mentioned to a friend, an expert swimmer, that I was not very good at swimming. As a goodbye present he generously offered to give me swimming lessons. The first day of lessons came; we changed, he got in the water, but I kept talking to him from the concrete edge of the pool. "Juan!" he shouted. "To learn to swim you have to get into the water!" To understand actions you must *do* them.

Our signifying actions in worship are human actions, and so they are *physical*, for worship involves doing something in a place, decorating it perhaps, moving, engaging objects, gesturing, washing, eating, anointing, keeping silence, singing, and speaking—all things related to or done by our bodies. We can't very well gather to only think or talk about God, without anything tangible. If we could, the church would be something like a network of preserved brains. We need visible, tangible, physical actions in order to have liturgy. And this is connected to one of God's real mysteries, the Incarnation.

It is precisely thanks to God becoming human in Jesus that we can and must use physical signs to live our spiritual lives physically, audibly, visually, as limbs of his body in history. And so in worship the spiritual is also physical, just as in Christ his humanity and divinity are united. Pope Leo the Great who wrote that "what had been visible in Christ (his humanity) before the Ascension passed over into the sacraments of the Church."[3]

Since the liturgy is embodied, it is also a practice, a doing, engaged in by the whole congregation and not only its leaders. It is not—despite our inherited architecture—a "show" to be watched passively, nor is it only the shared reading of texts. It is something we do again and again as a Christian community, a practice in both senses of the

---

3 Leo the Great, "Sermon on the Ascension," 74. Retrieved February 27, 2022, from https://www.newadvent.org/fathers/360374.htm.

term. We *do* it, and at the same time we are practicing something to get it right: life with God, here on earth, when God's reign arrives. We are not only remembering past events in liturgy, but also rehearsing life with God today as we act out what life in God's reign will look and feel like. We are re-membering the future too.

Anthropologists assure us that in our ritual practice, our attitudes about life, the world, God, ourselves, and each other are being shaped—that is *formed* in us as ever more mature Christians, precisely through our practice. It is not only our ideas that are being formed; our bodies too are being taught how to gather, show reverence, listen, express reconciliation, offer the fruits of our life and labor, and give thanks. Anthropologists also point out that in religious ritual we rehearse what our communities consider to be of greatest significance to the community: in our case, the life of the reign of God, not as it will be in heaven but, as we pray in the Lord's Prayer, when it arrives here among us on earth.[4]

Engaging the Signs

So, you may well ask, "What does it take to be able to "read" the sign-actions and enter into them?" St. Thomas Aquinas, commenting on the classical definition of

---

4 Stephen S. Wilbricht, *Rehearsing God's Just Kingdom: The Eucharistic Vision of Mark Searle* (Collegeville, MN: The Liturgical Press, 2013).

sacraments as signs that effect, or bring about, God's grace in the worshipper, pointed out the importance of the worshipper's *proper disposition in faith*. We are, however, so accustomed to the word "faith" meaning the intellectual assent of our minds to an unprovable claim that we have lost the full meaning of the Greek term *pistis,* which means a "trusting allegiance," closer to "the trust of my heart," or "confidently relying on someone." This meaning may be best captured by our use of the word followed by "in," as in, "I have faith *in* you." Faith in this sense is the trust of the whole person in the object of trust who is God. You may have noticed, for example, that in the Creed we do not say, "We believe *that*" but rather "we believe *in.*"

So we may say that the sacraments are signs of God's grace offered to worshippers as they put their trust in God and in what God is offering through sign-actions, persons, and objects. Our ability to engage a sacramental sign always involves trust in God and God's action through our worship and what it signifies. If we have no trust in God, nor care at all who Jesus Christ was, if we consider the Eucharist to be simply another social gathering, and do not have any trust in its ability to manifest Christ among us, the sacrament is still the sacrament, but we are not be open to the grace that it brings about in us. *God's sacramental self-offering to us is there all along but God will not force us to accept the free gift of grace.* We must open the door with a trusting faith. We trust in what the signs make present, holding in tension *both* the knowledge that we are engaging signs, *and* at the same time experiencing the realities that they point to. Aquinas also added that the sacraments "effect grace by meaning." That is, when a sign has no meaning for us, its ability to bring about the grace it signifies passes us by unawares. In this sense, then, the sacraments are not machines.

In sum, liturgy is made up of sign-actions, which are at the same time the realities they make present. This was beautifully explained to me by six-year-old Stephanie in the wisest sacramental insight I have ever heard. When I asked her, "Tell me, what is the bread we eat here?" She proudly recited, "The bread is the Body of Christ." Then she hesitated, thinking, and added, "Well, it isn't, but it is." We can now fill out the definition of sacraments a bit further:

Sacraments are visible, physical, Christian sign-actions through which God's own divine life is shared with the participants given their proper disposition in trusting faith.

Meaning and Literalism

Being an ensemble of sign-actions, Christian liturgy offers meaning to those who participate in it. If not, it is meaningless.

This presents a very real challenge to any conversation about liturgical formation today. For over twenty centuries, our sign-actions, objects, and gestures have gradually become increasingly opaque, less and less transparent until even people with theological training can entirely miss what the sign means. Or, sensing that ritual must refer to something, they make up meanings out of whole cloth to fill the gap. As we have seen, however, signs work best when they easily and without explanation lead us to the signified. So *the sign-actions in worship need to be clear and graspable by those who are worshipping.*

When human signs are working well, they do not need much, if any, explanation. For instance, we should not have to explain that in communion, we are sharing food and drink. It should be obvious. What needs reflection or unpacking is what sharing this meal means to those who engage in it. But frequently, leaders in formation are so busy explaining that it *is* real food and drink, that we have no time to share *what the meal means to us*, and to our communities. It is precisely because the sign-actions of our liturgy are not clear that some enthusiastic clergy want to *explain* the signs employing tools like "instructed Eucharists." They often refer to this practice as "catechesis"—an explanation of things unknown. The problem is that explaining a hug, as we saw above, is a lousy way to come to its meaning!

Additionally, our contemporaries are increasingly unable to think poetically but are driven to think only literally, making our experience of liturgical sign-actions difficult

21

and flat. The water of baptism, for example, often remains just water, bearing no further freight of meaning. We cannot experience it as the waters of the Flood, the Red Sea, and the River Jordan as its blessing prayer suggests. For those with a literal bent, eating and drinking bread and wine in memory of Jesus is just that: the bread is just bread, the wine just wine. They do not re-present or make present Christ, whose Body we are as a community. When experienced literally, the water, bread, and wine only make *themselves* present, and thus do not work as signs of anything. In today's world, where many consider only scientific data "real," it is a challenge for many to see something as *a sign holding a surplus of meaning that engages the whole person*. For early Christians, however, the sign was pregnant with layers of meaning. What to our ancestors was a world shining with many meanings can be perceived as one-dimensional and flat to contemporary Christians. This is a very real challenge to liturgical formation.

In sum, liturgy is a form of human religious ritual, a type of behavior in a time and place set apart and related to God, ourselves, and the rest of the world. It is made up of actions, people, and objects that work as physical, embodied signs pointing to mysteries, to God, the incarnation, the resurrection, the Church and Christ, and God's reign. Furthermore, these signs "work" precisely through our doing them. When they work well as signs, they are full of meaning, and as we engage them with trusting faith, we receive God's grace.

Questions for Discussion

1. List several non-religious rituals that you and your family engage in outside of church. What do they mean to you?

2. Besides the liturgy celebrated in church, what other examples of public service is your parish involved in?

3. Name some examples of the signs involved in the eucharistic liturgy. What do some of these mean *to you*?

4. What are some aspects of the liturgy that baffle you?

5. How has your participation in the liturgy formed you as a Christian over the years?

2 ▪ How Does the Liturgy Form Us in Christian Faith and Life?

Whenever my niece complains that what we do in church is meaningless to her, I sit up and take notice. Her expectation that this event we call liturgy should be meaningful is right on target, for if our liturgical actions, and the persons and objects involved, are signs, we should expect them to hold some meaning for us and should be forming us in something! Let us then consider how liturgical formation takes place, first and foremost, in and through our *experience* of worship.

First, we will acknowledge the human need for meaning in life. Do we not recognize that a meaningless life is intolerable to us? We will also look at how an ensemble of actions, persons, and objects working as signs engages us in a process of meaning-making. These meanings may be very personal or widely shared through the centuries, and of course they can be emotional or intellectual, or both. Finally, since meaning is always meaning-to-someone, and human beings are shaped by our cultures, the meanings of worship are also related to the cultures among which it takes place.

The Human Need for Meaning

Sometimes our human need for meaning is so strong that it gets out of hand. My liturgy professor, Louis Weil, used to tell his students the following story. During a graduation ceremony at a seminary, Louis was vested in an academic gown and since he was going to assist in the distribution of communion, he wore a white stole as well. It was very hot, and at one point he pushed his stole away from the back of his neck to cool off. Afterwards, an eager gentleman approached him with a question: "Father, what is the meaning of pushing back the stole?"

"*That it's hot!*" Louis shot back.

The anecdote points to something important. Human beings expect rituals to mean something. Perhaps too much so, as in this case, but this is entirely normal, for we humans are in a sense meaning-making creatures. Humans expect and look for meaning in life. We should thus expect that people engaged in worship will do the same—so much so that when meaning is not readily available we assume it should be—or make it up entirely!

By meaning, we often refer to "making sense"—that is, intelligibility. We want to make sense of our experience— from the birth of a child to the death of a spouse—in such a way as to integrate it into the rest of our lives. The term itself, "meaning," implies something being in the middle as a mediation, or a connector of one thing to another. The meaning of a hug, for example, is the connection between the hug, what it expresses, and my life. The hug means or mediates or expresses love, friendship, closeness—not by talking about it but by enacting it. Its meaning is *embodied:* we experience it first, immediately, even before we think and talk about it.

Many people expect meanings to have been already *given,* established, lying "out there" waiting for us to grasp them in a sermon, a library, or the internet. And so we ask Google what a term means in another language and Google translate pops up with a (not very good) answer. Or we ask the Book of Common Prayer and find the answer in the Catechism. In this sense, meaning is given, found, and received. But there is a different kind: We can actually *make* meaning.

If I ask a mother, "What was your daughter's baptism like for you? What did it mean to you?" she might say, "Oh it was lovely. Being able to dress her afterwards in my grandmothers' christening gown was so moving!" What was meaningful for the mother? Dressing her daughter in her grandmother's baptismal gown. For her, the meaning of baptism was associated with a family commitment to baptism signified in the baptismal gown that had been passed from one generation to the next.

Types of Meaning

If the mother wanted to find a *given* meaning, she could, of course, look up Holy Baptism in the Catechism of the Book of Common Prayer in order to find out what the

Episcopal Church thinks it means. There she would find the theological meaning or significance of baptism for us as Episcopalians. Let's be careful: *we should not assume that her meaning is less important than what is mentioned in the prayer book.* It may or may not agree with the meaning that the rest of us as a larger community have developed over centuries, in which case conversation may be encouraged and sought out. And yet even the theological meanings of the liturgy arose and developed over centuries precisely out of personal meanings shared, discussed, and argued over until we could come to a more or less shared meaning.

Furthermore, ritual is made up of signs with *multiple* meanings, both communal as well as personal. The Eucharist, for example, is the memorial of Jesus's Last Supper, but also of his death and resurrection, the pledge of the reign of God, the messianic banquet, and much more. Baptism is a purifying bath, but also a new birth, a death and resurrection, the forgiveness of sins, and our incorporation into Christ's Body, the Church, all at the same time. All of these dimensions of meaning are found in these two sacraments, and much more. And these are just the shared meanings developed over centuries. The personal meanings may well be as varied as there are worshippers!

You may have noticed that the mother quoted above did not say the meaning was an abstract idea about baptism. She went straight to the emotional component of the event for her: it was *moving* to see her daughter in her grandmother's baptismal gown. For her, the event did not have an abstract meaning. It moved her and therefore had a certain claim or importance in her life. This points to another facet of liturgical meaning: it is not only intellectual but also emotional, and thus informs and makes a claim on our lives. So it is fair to say that the meanings available in worship are much more varied and widespread than what a theology student reads in a library.

Culture

Furthermore, meaning is always meaning to *someone,* and that someone is always a concrete, specific person shaped by, living and breathing in, a culture, a society, with its historical and socioeconomic ways of living in the world. So liturgical meaning is always meaning to culturally-shaped persons. And this brings up the relationship between liturgy and cultures.

The liturgical action is meaningful to someone specific, not to generic human beings across cultures and languages but to concrete persons. For there is not, as far as we know, any human being on this planet that is not part of and formed by a culture. We cannot assume, therefore, that the meanings found or developed by Northern Europeans in their liturgical practice over twenty centuries will be exactly the same as the liturgical meaning to an indigenous person in Brazil. There are no generic human beings, only concrete persons formed by their culture, customs, language, and understanding of the world. We might go to the library and find the meaning of the Eucharist taught by St. Augustine in fourth-century North Africa—agree with it or not—and in the process, further develop *our* own meaning. But it is *Augustine's* understanding—and maybe, after we have wrestled with it, it might become *our* meaning.

Meaning, therefore, does not exist disconnected from culturally formed persons. Even the doctrinal, shared meanings of Christian worship were originally personal and culturally informed by Europeans, Western Asians, and North Africans, becoming over time meanings to us as a community—a community always in the midst of a culture. This is why, for example, it is so crucial to understand a biblical text—or a liturgical practice—in its original historical and cultural context, lest we project ours into it and misconstrue its original meaning entirely.

Finally, shared meanings are extremely important, for at the very least they have stood the test of centuries. That does not take away, however, the need for each Christian today to develop their own *personal* meanings in worship in conversation with our shared meanings developed over the centuries. This is what the phrase "liturgical formation" refers to: the shaping of a mature Christian over time, through the process of engaging the meanings found in worship. In a very real sense, this is precisely what every seminary professor hopes for: that students will develop their personal theological meanings through a fairly intense process of bringing their life experience into dialogue with Christian tradition.

Rehearsal of the Reign of God

In the last chapter I mentioned that liturgy works as a rehearsal of our life with God as a community: the reign or kingdom of God as we imagine it will be when it fully arrives here on earth. The notion that the liturgy is a rehearsal of the reign of God, developed by Roman Catholic liturgical scholar Mark Searle, is important: not only because practicing something forms us, but because we are practicing the reign of God as if it had already arrived.

The practice or "rehearsal" of the reign of God in liturgy forms and equips us to live in it, instilling in us a shared worldview and ethos. By "worldview," we mean an overall sense of the world, in this case, a Christian worldview. Ethos is the way or style of being and behaving in that world—the "Christian way," if you will. Elements such as the goodness of creation, the reality of its incompleteness and need for healing, the gracious self-emptying of God to become human, Christ's proclamation of God's gracious will to give us the reign, his healings and miracles, his free forgiveness without any requirements, and his final victory over evil and death through his death and ongoing life—all these aspects of our faith inform our vision of what the world is like and how to live in it as disciples. The announcement is clear at the beginning of the Holy

Eucharist: "Blessed be his [God's] kingdom, now and forever. Amen" (Book of Common Prayer 355). We are now in the reign or kingdom of God.

This sense of the way the world is and how to live in it with God, in God's reign, is practiced again and again in our liturgy, and it is in this sense that liturgical theologians often refer to the liturgy, especially the Eucharist, as the rehearsal of God's coming reign of love, forgiveness, justice, and peace. Furthermore, it is in light of this liturgical rehearsal of the life of the reign of God that we can know when we fall short of it. The liturgy, therefore, also integrates our failures to live in the reign of God through confession, forgiveness, and renewals. The liturgy has us *practice* living in the reign of God, and in this way liturgy *itself* is formative, even though much of this may take place unawares.

We engage in this rehearsal of the coming reign of God *as if* it had already arrived here among us. In it our actions, persons, and objects, working as signs, enable us to see and feel God's loving will to heal all of creation, and to know, in our bones, how God's reign will look and feel when it arrives fully among us. Equipped by this vision, and familiar with the reign and how it feels to live in it, we can go out into the world to recognize God already at work in it, and join in.

First Order Liturgical Formation

Theologians like to say that there are two different "orders" or types of theology: First there is the *experience of God* in prayer and worship itself. This is primal, "first order" theology. Then there is *reflection upon* our experience of faith in prayer. This is "second order" theology. We can say the same about liturgical formation: first order liturgical formation takes place as we participate fully and consciously in the liturgy. Thus, our participation in the Eucharist actively and consciously every Sunday is itself liturgical formation. Liturgy, therefore, is the first and most foundational occasion for the formation of Christians. What we do in worship, and how we do it, shapes or forms us.

Second order liturgical formation consists of reflecting, individually and as communities, on our liturgical experience. Both types of liturgical formation are extremely important and both together are what we mean by liturgical formation. But both present us with very real challenges today.

In the case of first order liturgical formation—the liturgical experience itself—we face today what I call the challenge of opacity: over the centuries, what our actions, persons, and objects meant originally to the participants has been obscured so that the meanings of the signs are not as clear as they could be. In order to grasp how far we have come away from a liturgical experience needing little explanation, it may be helpful to visit a second-century Eucharist in Rome.

They have come together from all over the place, these thirty or so people gathered this Saturday evening (already Sunday according to Jewish time)—some walking in from the countryside to gather at Simplicius's house. Usually they would all bring food to share, but tonight they are being fed by Simplicius and his servants, recently baptized as a single household. For Simplicius, this is not only hospitality, but a *leiturgia*: an action taken for the good of the people, in this case, the gathered church. The event is also considered, in Roman cultures around the Mediterranean, to be a *sacrifice*, that is, a sacred thing, a sacred offering to a god.

First, they wash their hands upon entering an open garden surrounded by colonnades. There are too many to fit into the dining room with its Roman reclining couches, so instead they arrange themselves here and there in groups around small tables where the food will be placed. The meal—like all meals of ordinary people at the time—consists mostly of bread, wine, and vegetables, raw, pickled, and cooked. Meat is not usually eaten for it is associated with pagan temples. Tonight, however, Simplicius is also generously providing fish from the Tiber River.[5]

The one who presides (known as the supervisor or *episkopos*) welcomes all. If the group is particularly Jewish, the Jewish thanksgiving is said over broken bread and a cup of wine and both are shared. They eat with gusto, catching

---

5 Andrew B. McGowan, *Ancient Christian Worship* (Grand Rapids, MI: Baker Publishing, 2014).

up with each other. As the meal comes to a close the one who presides stands, and following Roman custom, offers a solemn toast in honor of their God, Jesus Christ. She thanks God for sending Christ to us, as teacher and liberator, and prays for the Spirit to come to all, and for the reign of God to arrive soon (*Didache*, 9–10). This very basic prayer/toast would eventually, by the fourth century, also recall Christ's death and resurrection and invoke the Holy Spirit upon them and those gathered—what today we know as the Eucharistic Prayer or Great Thanksgiving.

The "toast" began the second part of the meal: the *symposium* or drinking party. Writing in the third century, Tertullian mentioned that they do not drink *too* much, for they are aware that they are at a holy event; besides, they stand up individually and offer a song or a psalm, or maybe a message from God. Being in Rome, some speak in foreign languages that need to be translated. Perhaps something is read from the Jewish Bible, and from the already available "good news" of God in Jesus, or the letter of Paul to the Christians in Rome. The *episkopos* then offers words encouraging all to live like proper disciples of Christ. People stand and pray for this and that, including the emperor and other officials. Eventually the *diakonoi,* the servants, start clearing up the place, sending the eucharistic leftover bread and wine to those who could not attend.

There are several things that are noticeable in this description, mostly by their *absence.* First, it is a full, not a token meal; also, although to us this liturgy may look fairly informal, it is in fact structured by the Roman customs of guilds and other affinity groups meeting over meals in honor of their patron god. There are no hierarchical distinctions; only the special roles of the *episkopos* or supervisor and the *diakonoi* or servants. People participate fully, speaking up and to each other as they wish. There is singing, maybe with accompanying instruments; there may be dancing. There is a reading, a sermon or interpretation of the scriptural reading, and a solemn toast or thanksgiving that will eventually become the Eucharistic Prayer as we know it today. There is also no "moment of consecration" or words of institution, although Paul has already taught, a hundred years earlier, that the gathered church *is* the Body of Christ, and the gospels include passages about meals in which the risen Christ shows up and is recognized.

There are of course, no pews, vestments, or special accouterments. A napkin is not yet called a purificator, nor a place mat a corporal. The bread is obviously bread—one loaf, broken and shared, showing that "Because there is one bread, we who are many are one body, for we all partake of the one bread" (1 Cor. 10:17).

What does this all mean *to this group*? Besides being an obviously religious event by Roman standards, the gathering is already considered to be evidence of the reign of God already here among us. This is not simply an abstraction or even a hope; *it is tangible and sensible*, already present in the way the participants relate to each other around a shared meal. Perhaps most saliently, it is so because the poor and hungry eat cheek by jowl with the comfortable; women with men; Greeks with Jews, foreigners with citizens, slaves with their masters. It is evidence of a new world, a new society, the reign of God. This regular practice in fact *formed* the participants in a Christian worldview and ethos, both as individuals and as communities, so they could live their daily life as if they were already in the reign of God, cooperating with God in the process of bringing it about.

Other than it being a sign of the reign of God, none of this needed to be *explained*. Since they all belonged to Roman culture, everyone knows that this is the meal of a group in honor of Christ their God, just as the blacksmith's guild gathered to eat in honor of Vulcan, and the midwives in honor of Juno. There is also no need to explain the obvious; no need to explain what a "host," a "corporal," a "purificator," a "chasuble" or "alb" were, for these did not yet exist in Christian worship. What *was* explored were rather the *real* mysteries: the Creator God and God's infinite love for creation, to the point of sending the Word to heal and free it from slavery to the powers that spread evil and death; the good news of the nearness of God's reign proclaimed by Jesus in deeds and words, and how he relates to the Hebrew Bible; the presence of the risen Christ among his Body, the Church, and his promise to return to establish God's reign fully here on earth. That is to say, what was explained—as we know from a few sermons—is what God is up to: liberating this world through Jesus's life, actions, teaching, death and resurrection from slavery to the powers of sin and death that harm and destroy the creatures of God, and how to live like a Christian in light of all this.

Beyond Explaining

This little description, I hope, makes something clear: *True liturgical formation is not about explaining vocabulary.* So why do so many people think it is? Perhaps we have not kept up with the process of making sure that our liturgical actions, people, and objects—and their vocabulary—are crystal clear. It really does not make much difference, spiritually, whether one calls the purificator by that term or refers to the "napkin" or, as my favorite Latina altar guild member calls it, "*el pañito,*" the little cloth! Not one bit. In fact some people, I fear, hang on to that terminology and brag about knowing it as if it made them somehow superior, defending its use as evidence of "mystery" when they really mean obfuscation or mystification.

In sum, as ritual, our liturgical actions, persons, and objects come together to form us in Christian worldview and ethos: a vision of the world and how to live in it as Christians, *when and if they are transparent.* But today this does not take place automatically. The very existence of "instructed liturgies'"—liturgies interrupted by explanations —is evidence that the signs are not always transparent; that the "hug" needs explaining. We cannot, and should not, of course, pretend that we are in the second century, but perhaps we can learn something about transparency in worship and the full and complete use of signs from the first Christians.

We have seen above how humans expect that liturgy, being a system of signs, will have meaning. We expect ritual to *mean something* so much so that when it does not, we can make up its meaning. We want the experience to "make sense" to integrate it into the rest of our lives.

Sometimes the meaning of the liturgical experience is not "given" and received, but created or constructed by the participant. This personal meaning may be emotional rather than intellectual, or it may have no connection to church teachings. Nevertheless, it is the participant's meaning. Additionally the liturgical signs may have *multiple theological and personal meanings*, which may be both intellectual and affective. Liturgical formation, then, is the process of allowing the words, actions, gestures, movements, music, artifacts, and architecture in worship to be fully meaningful and formative, and then supporting reflection upon the liturgical experience.

All this is to say that weekly participation in worship *is* primary liturgical formation. What we do in worship, and how we do it, shapes or forms us as Christians. True liturgical formation in Christian identity and purpose is not about explaining terms or actions. Rather, it is the experience of being with others in worship, the doing of worship.

Questions for Discussion

1. Give examples of signs in your everyday life (religious or not) and their meaning for you.
2. Think of a very personal meaning that the Eucharist has *for you* that you might not find in the prayer book.
3. How do you think the culture you belong to shapes or influences your experience of worship?
4. What, if anything, surprised you about the description of a third century Eucharist at Simplicius' house?

3 ▪ Why Is It Important to Reflect on Our Experience of the Liturgy?

The liturgy is a rich source of meanings. I say "meanings" in the plural because, as we've seen, the meanings of worship are multiple, personal and shared, intellectual and emotional, layered together in a rich, complex experience that can transform us and sustain us as we grow spiritually, individually, and as communities. These multiple layers of shared meaning join personal memories, for example, the very first time we ate and drank at Eucharist or that time during a long pandemic when we fasted from it. Because of this richness of liturgical meanings, it is important in liturgical formation to keep the personal meanings and the shared meanings in dialogue with each other, even though the process begins with the worship experience itself.

Let us now consider the second type of liturgical formation: reflection upon our liturgical experience, exploring and deepening the meaning of worship *for us* through reflection on our own liturgical experience of the sacraments in conversation with each other and with the treasure house of meanings that we have accumulated over centuries.

Professional theologians usually try to keep our personal experience out of the picture, for we are interested mainly in what the liturgical experience has meant over centuries, concentrating on the church's experience *as a community*. But we don't have to limit our reflection to the living tradition of the church's understanding. In fact, for formation to work deeply in us, we need to reflect on our experience of worship, preferably in dialogue with the church's tradition. Though rather rare today, this reflection upon the liturgical experience was taken very seriously in the early church.

The Early Church's Second Order Liturgical Formation

The New Testament, its various books written between approximately 50 and 120 CE, already contained reflection upon the church's experience of worship. Many passages refer to the meals practiced by the first Christians and possibly to songs and scripture passages mentioned in them. In 1 Corinthians, Paul describes such a meal in some detail, and the gospels mention post-resurrection meals—usually on Sunday—in which the disciples recognize Jesus present among them. Early sermons and other writings do so as well.

By the mid-fourth century, however, as crowds of converting pagans began to fill the large basilicas built by the emperor Constantine, Christian leaders wanted to make sure that new Christians, formed in Roman values and practices, understood and practiced what they were getting into *before* their incorporation into the church. And so they developed a prolonged period of preparation for baptism, confirmation, and Eucharist, which came to be called the catechumenate.

During this period seekers would "marinate" in the Word of God, learn to worship fully and consciously, develop skills for prayer and spiritual growth, and serve the poor and needy. Finally the great day came, and they were incorporated into the household of God, the Body of Christ, as full members. Throughout, the emphasis had been on the Word and how it was illuminating and transforming their lives. Now, after their washing in the font, anointing, and first communion, they would explore the meanings of the sacraments they had just experienced, the nature of the church, and its mission.

You may wonder why these meanings of the sacraments were not explained *before* their baptism, but *after*, reflecting on their *experience*. The reason is simple: It would be silly for a couple to discuss the meaning of their honeymoon before their wedding. *Experience is of the essence in liturgical formation.* In order to reflect on the liturgy and its meanings, we must, as we saw above, "jump into the water" and experience it first. Then we can reflect on our experience.

In the fourth century this process, called "leading into the mysteries" (mystagogy), lasted the full seven weeks of Easter. During those weeks, the bishop unfolded for the newly-baptized the various meanings of what they had just experienced liturgically. In the fourth century, for example, Cyril of Jerusalem began his sermons with these words:

> Since I well knew that seeing is far more persuasive than hearing, I waited till now, so that you would be open to my words from your *experience*, and I might lead you by the hand into the brighter and more fragrant meadow of the Paradise before us; for you have received the more sacred Mysteries, after having been found worthy of divine and life-giving Baptism.[6]

Let's take a closer look, not in Jerusalem but in Rome. It is the Wednesday after Easter Day at the baptismal hall next to St. John's Basilica at the Lateran. The recently baptized members have gathered in a room next to the waist-deep octagonal font (which survives to this day). They are meeting with their bishop, who had baptized, confirmed, and welcomed them to communion the previous Saturday night, at the Easter Vigil. They would continue to meet every week for seven weeks to explore the meanings of the liturgical actions. The bishop points again and again to an action—for example, immersion in the font—and discusses how it is an imitation or likeness of Christ's death and

---

6 Cyril of Jerusalem, *Catechetical Lectures*, 19. Retrieved February 22, 2022, from https://newadvent.org/fathers/3101.htm. Emphasis mine.

resurrection, often marveling that though Christ's death was real, we are freed from bondage to sin and death by a *likeness* of that death without need for bloodshed. That is, immersion is a *sign* of death and resurrection. He might do the same with other parts of the liturgy, for example, the giving of milk mixed with honey to the baptized as a sign of their entry into the promised land. Informing these sermons is a sense of wonder at the marvelous ways in which the liturgical actions embody and express biblical passages.

Modern Teaching

Today it is tempting (for me at least) to lecture for seven weeks to increasingly bored parishioners, but thankfully the art of teaching has come a long way since new Christians were subjected to lectures. Today, teachers must take very seriously the student's interests, passions, existential issues, and questions. Teaching and learning are not, in this view, simply knowledge moving from a teacher's overflowing brain to a student's empty head, but something that is actively built up *by the student* with the assistance of the teacher, who works rather as a resource. This presents a very real challenge to those of us who grew up thinking that teaching consists of transferring information from one brain to another. It is much better, we now know, for the student to be actively involved, not only in the choice of topics *that matter to her*, but even in the ways in which these are explored and addressed. Throughout, the more the student is in the driver's seat, and the more the teacher becomes a *companion and resource* in the process, the better.

Besides, since the meanings of worship are first of all meanings to individual worshippers, that is the best place to begin. The newly baptized, confirmed, or received share their experiences of the rites and what they meant to them, and as this is shared, we can assist them in conversing with our tradition and its understandings of what took place. My book *A House of Meanings*[7] is designed as a tool to assist parishioners in exploring the meaning of the sacraments, beginning before Holy Week and progressing weekly through Easter to Pentecost. In a sense it is an "Easter Program." It may be engaged individually or in parish groups or forums, during this time or, with some adaptation, any other time of the year.

Although most members of the clergy, I am sure, feel a responsibility to teach as called for in our ordination vows, we often limit this to preaching. But preaching, as essential as it is, is only one way of teaching. As we have seen above, the early church had another: the exploration of the meaning of the liturgical signs.

Many clergy are used to talking—and talking a lot!—and this can prove to be a challenge if liturgical formation

---

7 Juan M. C. Oliver, *A House of Meanings: Christian Worship in Plain Language* (New York: Church Publishing, 2019).

rightly begins with the people's experience of and reflection on worship and the sacraments. This process asks clergy and chatty teachers to listen first. And it may well be that a lay catechist or teacher should lead these gatherings in which people reflect on their experience of the liturgy. Occasionally, of course, the group will have a pressing theological or historical concern, and a lay leader may invite a member of the clergy in for a special session to give something closer to a "class," preferably at a different time from the regular reflection group's meetings.

In any case, whoever leads, lay or ordained, must bring excellent listening skills, noticing what the person is saying, encouraging it, and when appropriate—*if it emerges*—connecting it to the tradition, and if seeking deeper teaching, perhaps with an invited speaker. She will, of course, also need to encourage the shy and gently manage those who want to give speeches, dominating the conversation.

Leading Liturgical Reflection

Instead of beginning with a list of topics to be covered, and pouring all that information into the passive students week by week, the leader asks the most basic, fundamental question: How does your liturgical experience (of baptism, confirmation, reception, Eucharist) relate to *your* life? And since "liturgical experience" is a huge category, taking a whole lifetime to explore, in liturgical formation the question becomes, initially, "What was the liturgical experience like *for you*?" Still a very open question, and so I have found that it helps to divide it into smaller questions, for example, reflecting on a baptism: "What was it like to wade into the font? To be immersed three times, in the name the Father, Son, and Holy Spirit? To come out for air? To be anointed generously with chrism by the priest and your sponsors? To be dressed in new clothes? To receive a lit candle, the light of Christ? What was it like for you (maybe for the first time) to pray with us for the world and the church? To receive Holy Communion? To be sent into the world to heal it?"

Even if the baptism is celebrated minimally without such amplitude, the leader can adapt the questions to the way the ritual took place. I have found that taking a video of the ritual, usually as a gift to the family, and playing it by bits during these sessions is very helpful. It also helps to hold these sessions in a festive context, maybe including a meal: it is Easter, after all! Additionally, I have usually invited anyone from the congregation who wishes to come, observe, and listen to the conversation for they too were part of the liturgical experience of the group. In the process, the "old timers" discover facets of their own liturgical experience that they had never noticed or named before.

I have also found something wonderful: often the newly baptized (or confirmed or received) come up with meanings that, entirely unawares, echo back to great theologians of our tradition. "I was amazed not to feel shame about my body," a woman told us one Easter, echoing Cyril of Jerusalem:

> As soon as you entered, you put off your tunic; and this was an image of putting off the old person and her deeds. Having stripped yourselves, you were naked; . . . O wondrous thing! You were naked in the sight of all, [of the same sex] and were not ashamed; for truly you bore the likeness of the first-formed Adam, who was naked in the garden, and was not ashamed.[8]

Notice here one important thing: Bishop Cyril is not going directly to the *theological* meaning of baptism. Rather, he uses an experience—being naked—and connects it to Eden. There is a sense of wonder in his talk, wonder at the parallel between baptismal candidates and Adam and Eve. The just baptized and Adam and Eve are *analogous* (similar) to each other, and similarity, as we saw earlier, is one of the roads that lead to finding meaning—the connection of one thing to another.

Another candidate, an African American teenage girl, said about being anointed: "I thought: Oh! This is how David must have felt, going from shepherd to king!" A mechanic said: "I felt like I was becoming what I was eating, Christ!"—echoing Augustine's "Behold who you are, become what you receive." It is a great gift for a new

---

8 Cyril of Jerusalem, *Catechetical Lectures*, 20.

Christian to learn that she is already a theologian, actively finding meaning in the liturgical event while at times even channeling insights from our ancient tradition.

In congregations where I have served, these liturgical reflection groups meet during Easter. For seven weeks, they explore the two great sacraments—baptism and Eucharist—and in the light of these, other sacraments as well, ending up with a conversation about the Spirit and the mission of the church to the world, closer to Pentecost. If the larger number of baptisms take place at other parts of the year, however, the "leading into the mysteries" conversations may as easily be held after that time. Moreover, once a congregation gets used to these conversations, they begin to engage in them during the rest of the year.

History and Theology

And what about theology, you may well ask? I do keep a list of topics that I hope will come up, and sometimes gently lead in that direction if they are not; but by and large all the main topics get covered not as abstractions but as *discoveries made by the new disciple-theologians* reflecting upon their experience.

Still, some participants in the reflection group will want more history and theology of the liturgy than others. This is why my *A House of Meanings* includes the history and theology of Holy Week, the Easter Vigil, and the great

Fifty Days of Easter, ending with Pentecost, to provide the leader and participants with a sketch of the history and theology of the sacraments and their meanings for us as a community, especially during the first six centuries.

Questions for Discussion

1. What surprised you about the description of a fourth-century process of reflection upon the experience of baptism, anointing, and Eucharist?

2. If you had to lead something similar today, what changes would you make?

3. Think of an example of how you have reflected upon your experience of worship. What did you come up with?

4. Reflecting upon a particular segment of the Eucharist, what does that action mean *to you*?

4 ▪ What Does Liturgical Formation Look Like in the Church Today?

If liturgical formation takes place first of all within the liturgy, but also through reflection on our experience of it, *why is this so rare in our church today?* After all, we experience worship very often; hopefully we also stop and reflect on it at least now and then. Combined, this almost total absence of these two modes of liturgical formation conspires to turn us into a community unaware of who we are, what we do ritually, and how it affects our lives. This double challenge is not written in stone, however; it can be addressed, and must, if we want to let the liturgy itself and our reflection upon it to form us.

Liturgical formation, both in and through worship as well as through reflection upon it, presents a serious challenge for the Episcopal Church today. At best, it is often confused with liturgical explaining—of liturgical colors or the meaning of different words (for example, "purificator"). That is not liturgical *formation;* it is simply liturgical *information.*

Let us first consider the ways in which our liturgical signs—the actions, persons, and objects involved in worship—have become opaque to the point that what they refer to is not evident to the participants. I will offer some practical ideas towards remedying the situation, and then proceed to tackle the almost total absence of deliberate, organized reflection on our liturgical experience in our congregations, providing some possible remedies taken from both the early church and our best modern teaching practices.

In order to begin to address this double challenge we first have to be aware of it and name it. So let us ask ourselves, why can what we do in liturgy be baffling and in need of explanation? Secondly, what can we do about it, other than gifting all members with pocket liturgical dictionaries? Thirdly, why is reflection and conversation upon our experience of worship almost totally absent in our congregations? And then, what might we be able to do in order to incorporate reflection upon our experience of liturgy in the formational programs of the congregation? With these questions and their answers in hand, we can offer some ways of moving ahead to improve our liturgical formation, as both individuals and as communities.

An Opaque Liturgy

From time to time some very committed and pastoral clergy, sensitive and responsible, try to explain what appears to be obscure in our ritual actions, objects, persons, and vocabulary. They occasionally hold forums on liturgical terms or the history of liturgical objects and actions, to explain, for example, that a host is bread, or that the paten is a plate.

As we saw earlier, however, explaining obscurities is not liturgical formation, but sharing information. There's nothing wrong with it, of course, but it is merely explaining things that the student does not understand. For example, an aging hippie once asked me: "Why do we call the psalm a 'gradual' psalm when we do not say it slowly?" A good question that merited this response: "A cantor used to sing the psalm while climbing, each step—a *gradius*—leading up to the pulpit."

Earlier I compared the nature of liturgy as an ensemble of signs to an expressive gesture like a hug embodying and expressing an attitude or feeling. Increasingly, however, I find that many a congregant stands stiff in the "hug" of liturgy, utterly in the dark about what is going on in worship. At best, they may have an inkling that worship is praise of God, and they are right, but it is so much more! Some cannot stand the itch, and actively try to find out. Or a parishioner may read a book or attend a forum on the topic. Most, however, simply go along assuming perhaps that they are not supposed to know what all this means, since it is a "mystery" or what is simply "expected" of people who worship regularly.

Like any human action repeated over thousands of years, Christian worship has come to contain actions, words, phrases, and objects that increasingly may seem unclear, puzzling to increasing numbers of people. This is not surprising, for any sign system traveling through two millennia, world-wide cultures, and diverse places and geographies is bound to become opaque and hard to decipher. These shifts in cultures, geographies, and societies twist and turn not only the meanings of our words but of our liturgical actions, persons, and objects as well. So it is not surprising that our sign-actions have become unintelligible to some of us and certainly to non-Christians.

Did you know, for example, that the word "sin," from the Anglo Saxon *synne*, is related to crime and criminality? This shading is not, however, contained in the Greek *hamartía* (missing the bull's eye, error, mistake), nor in the Latin *peccatum* (a stumbling, tripping, or falling). The mere act of translating *hamartía* into *synne* involved a cultural interpretation and a shift in its meaning. Actions, too, suffer the same fate. What used to be an immersion in water graphically expressing death and new life and a sign of the transformation of the new Christian, came to be a sweet little rite for family and friends celebrating the birth of a baby with a mere sprinkling of water on the head. Or what once was a full shared meal giving evidence, here and now, of the reign of God already sprouting among us became a *symbol* of a meal, even as the reign was increasingly kept at arm's length until it ended up in "heaven."

Additionally, since ritual is naturally conservative, wanting to show us "how it is done" under the rubric of "this is how we have always done it," it also conspires against change and development unless we make a special effort to keep the signs fresh. An example comes to mind: the liturgical changes of the sixteenth-century English Reformation.

Reformation Transparency

Headed by Thomas Cranmer, the writer of the first two Books of Common Prayer, the English reformers of the sixteenth century tried to bring the liturgy closer to their original transparency and power, and not only by worshipping in the vernacular, the language of the people. They did so also by rethinking the actions, persons, and objects that work as signs. So, for example, by the time of the second Book of Common Prayer (1552), Cranmer and his successors had taken out the marble altars set up against the east wall and replaced them with actual dining tables, placed either in mid chancel or even in the middle of the nave, for the communicants to stand or kneel around. And to stress that the Eucharist is the shared meal of a community and encourage people who for centuries were unaccustomed to receiving communion, they invited them to approach the table before the Confession:

> You that doe truly and earnestly repente you of youre synnes, and bee in love and charitie with

your neighbours, and entende to heade a newe lyfe, folowyng the commaundments of god, and walking from henceforth in his holy waies: Drawe nere and take this holy Sacramente to youre comfort: make your humble confession to almightie god, before this congregacion here gathered together in his holy name, mekely knelyng upon your knees.[9]

Those receiving communion would kneel around the Holy Table through the Confession of Sin, the Eucharistic Prayer, and reception of Holy Communion. Those not receiving were to go home instead. Likewise, the reformers soon did away with hosts, restoring the original use of bread and a generous flagon of wine. In fact Anglicans did not begin to use hosts widely until the early nineteenth century.

Sacramental Abbreviation

What Cranmer and the other reformers were trying to do was to *restore the signs to their original vigor*, for they had been, by the mid-sixteenth century, so abbreviated that they could not mean what they claimed to mean.

The history of Christian liturgy is rife with examples of abbreviation. By the year 205, for example, Tertullian reports

---

9 The Book of Common Prayer of 1552, 166. Cf., with the Book of Common Prayer 1979, 330.

that while the full eucharistic meal had been taking place on Saturday night (already Sunday by Jewish standards), some people began to stop by very early on Sunday on their way to work to pick up the eucharistic bread and wine from the night before. The full eucharistic meal on Saturday evening continued, but it was now increasingly attended mostly by the poor. Eventually the meal for and with the poor lost its eucharistic character and only the Sunday Eucharist, with readings and sermon survived. The full meal eventually became special fraternal meals in monasteries but they were not eucharistic.

Later, in the eleventh century, hosts were introduced either as a snub to the separated Eastern churches, which have always used leavened bread, or simply out of convenience as it is easier to preserve hosts than bread. This coincided with a growing sense of unworthiness to receive a sacrament, to the point that the Fourth Lateran Council in 1215 had to *oblige* Christians to receive communion at least once a year at Easter.

Around the same time the concept of "spiritual communion"—without any eating or drinking whatsoever—gained popularity, especially as medieval optical theory considered vision a mode of ingestion. And so the people, who often wandered to side altars to pray to the saints and venerate relics during Mass, or prayed the rosary, or gossiped and made business deals, rushed to the chancel at the sound of "sanctus bells," to peek through the chancel screen at the elevated host. It is no wonder that the Protestant Reformers wanted to refresh the sacramental signs.

These are only a few examples of attempts to restore vigor and meaning to the basic signs of the liturgy. In our day, many more may be possible, even necessary, if the ensemble of signs that is our liturgy is to mean directly, afresh, with as little explanation necessary as possible. And here's the point: *instead of explaining obscurities, we might try to make the signs clearer.* After all, who wants to spend time having to explain a hug? One way to do this is through the full and complete use of objects and actions in worship, without abbreviation.

Often abbreviations are defended in the name of efficiency. *Good liturgical practice, however, is never about efficiency.* Preoccupations about efficiency stem from attempts to boil down the liturgical action to its minimal essentials for it to still be, say, the Eucharist, or baptism, while dispensing with their fullest forms of celebration—what theologians call "the liturgical norm." In this way "efficiency" is always the enemy of our worship, unless of course one is referring to moments or details that are *not* signs, for example, a lector walking to the ambo, or a deacon setting the table, practical necessities to be done reverently but simply and efficiently.

Instead of asking ourselves, "What is the least we can get away with, or the fastest, most efficient way to do this?" we may ask ourselves, "How might we make this clearer, fuller, more ample, and richer?" The use of unabridged, full, and complete signs—actions, persons, and objects—in liturgy is a very good starting place towards making it less obscure. Otherwise, we risk shrinking the fullness of the sacramental signs, sucking out their ability to mean to the participant and so effect grace in the believer and having to say absurdities such as "a host is a symbol of bread" or "the Eucharist is a symbol of a meal." No. The Eucharist *is* a meal of food and drink, the fragment of an ancient Mediterranean meal, and a sign of the reign of God, the presence of Christ, and much more.

Thus, with an increased transparency of the signs clearly expressing what they mean, and needing as little explanation as possible, a congregation and its leaders will have more time for a pastoral exploration of the *real* mysteries in the liturgy: God, the Trinity, the Incarnation, the Gospel, the reign of God, and the church as Body of Christ sent to the world in mission.

Reflection upon Liturgy

The shrinking of liturgical signs is not, however, the only challenge before us. Tragically, reflection upon our experience of worship is almost completely absent from our common life as Episcopalians. In fact, conversations as a group exploring a topic are often equally absent in our congregations. Perhaps they may seem unnecessary in our individualistic culture for we so often reduce reality to "what is real for *me*," making religion into something private, with no communal aspects, either within the church community or the surrounding neighborhood. I need not go into how this destroys a congregation's identity as a community present in its neighborhood in witness to the gospel.

Additionally, with the end of Christendom, a very long age of Christian culture, we cannot count on secular culture to do the work of liturgical formation for us. In this way at least, *we are coming to resemble the early church more and more*. This means that we must pick up the challenge and develop skills and commit to liturgical *formation*. We have considered ways to do so within the worship experience. Now let us look at the challenge posed by reflecting on that experience, exploring two main ways in which we can engage in reflection as communities on the experience of worship: small group reflection and preaching.

The "Easter Program"

To assist in the formation of reflection groups in the parish, some basic "rules of the game" will create a safe space in which participants can feel secure and free to express themselves:

1. The liturgical reflection group is *not* a liturgical critique group.
2. All statements are "I" statements, like "I felt that . . . ."

3. All statements, even if contradictory, can "sit" next to each other. No one is wrong.

4. All statements are confidential and must not be repeated outside the group.

5. Every participant is the only judge of the degree to which she wishes to share something personal.

6. These rules are rehearsed often.

The basic elements of this process of "leading into the mysteries" begin with this: the participant is in the driver's seat, sharing reflection upon their experience. This reflection enters into dialogue with *our* experience as a community over centuries. In this way we facilitate an encounter between the participant's experience and contemporary living day to day *and* the ancient tradition of the church. It is neither liturgical antiquarianism nor a search for immediate "relevance." Rather, it explores the significance and meaning of what we do together as a worshipping assembly today and orients the participant toward life in the world, to join in the loving, liberating, and life-giving mission of the Triune God.

Finally, it is helpful to schedule these sessions regularly— for example every week at the same time and place. This is easier to do if the participants met and got to know each other during at least several weeks of preparation for their baptism, confirmation, or reception. So just as we have become familiar with Lenten programs, a congregation may develop an Easter program as well. This "Easter program" need not take place only during Easter. It may instead follow baptisms, confirmations, and receptions, held on the Feast of All Saints (November 1), or any other time.

In sum, reflection on the experience of the liturgy can take place in an organized way during the seven weeks of Easter, particularly when baptisms, confirmations, and receptions have taken place at the Easter Vigil or on Easter Day; or they can take place for seven weeks after any major celebration of the sacraments.

Liturgical Preaching

Besides the liturgical reflection group, there is another way of reflecting upon the meanings of worship: liturgical preaching. By the term I do not mean any preaching within the liturgy, but preaching that presents the connection between a liturgical action and the scriptures proclaimed. It is preaching about worship and how it makes present *now,* in this concrete congregation's life, events that took place and were written down two millennia ago or more. For example, the canons allow the readings in Year A to be proclaimed in Lent and Easter whenever there are baptisms at the Easter Vigil or on Easter Day. I have annotated the lectionary readings below, noting how they may connect to baptism and parts of the Holy Eucharist.

Easter Vigil and Easter Day: Romans 6:3–11, Psalm 114; Matthew 28:1–10. *Baptism as dying and rising in imitation of Jesus. Jesus meets the women and they recognize them. We recognize Christ in the newly baptized and each other.*

Second Sunday of Easter: Acts 2:14a, 22–32; Psalm 16; 1 Peter 1:3–9; John 20:19–31. *The fearful disciples recognize Jesus in the Upper Room. We recognize Jesus in our gathering to hear the Word of God, as the recently baptized have recognized the Lord in the Word throughout their preparation for baptism.*

Third Sunday of Easter: Acts 2:14a, 36–41; Psalm 116:1–3, 10–17; 1 Peter 1:17–23; Luke 24:13–35. *On the way to Emmaus, the disciples recognize Jesus at the breaking of the bread. We recognize Jesus in our shared meal that is the Holy Communion.*

Fourth Sunday of Easter: Acts 2:42–47; Psalm 23; 1 Peter 2:19–25; John 10:1–10. *Jesus the Good Shepherd: the sheep recognize the shepherd's voice. We recognize the voice of the Shepherd in our daily lives.*

Fifth Sunday of Easter: Acts 7:55–56; Psalm 31:1–5, 15–16; 1 Peter 2:2–10; John 14:1–14. *Jesus's farewell discourse: He is in the Father and the Father in him. We recognize that Jesus and the Father are one. Recognizing God in Jesus; Jesus as Lord.*

Sixth Sunday of Easter: Acts 17:22–31; Psalm 66:7–18; 1 Peter 3:13–22; John 14:15–21. *By keeping Jesus's commandments (love) the Father will send the Spirit. Exchanging the peace as an expression of the new commandment, love, and as reconciliation with each other.*

Seventh Sunday of Easter: Acts 1:6–14; Psalm 68:1–10, 33–36; 1 Peter 4:12–14; 5:6–11; John 17:1–11. *Jesus is one with the congregation. The congregation is the presence of Christ in the neighborhood.*

Pentecost: Acts 2:1–21 or Numbers 11:24–30; Psalm 104:25–35, 37; 1 Corinthians 12:3b–13 or Acts 2:1–21; John 20:19–23 or John 7:37–39. *The Spirited disciples go out to proclaim the gospel in deeds and words. The congregation is sent out with authority to announce the nearness of the reign, in deeds and, if necessary, words. Reflection on the sending rite from the post-communion through the dismissal.*

These are only some examples of how the readings proclaimed may be illustrated by different parts of the liturgy. They are not, of course, the only possible examples. Moreover, preachers need not limit themselves to Easter. It makes a lot of sense, for example, to connect the liturgical sacramental actions at baptisms (washing, immersing), confirmations (laying on of hands), Eucharists (giving thanks and sharing food and drink), marriages (joining of hands, vows) and ordinations (laying on of hands). One good example would be preaching about stewardship while illustrating the point by referring to the offertory procession—maybe on this occasion, a procession of all the people to the altar.

We have seen how liturgical formation, taking place first of all through our participation in worship, is necessarily complemented by a second form of formation: reflection upon the liturgical experience and the process of accompanying an individual or community as they explore and deepen the meaning of worship *for them*, through reflection on their own liturgical experience in dialogue with centuries of meaning for us, the gathered church.

We must stop claiming that the liturgy is supposed to be opaque, mysterious, and mystifying—a serious misunderstanding of what is meant by "mystery." To make the liturgy more transparent, I have suggested that congregations return to the full use of liturgical signs without any reductions based on a supposed "efficiency."

We have noted how formation through reflection on worship is almost completely absent from our common life. Through organized conversations on the sacramental liturgical experience, however, we can deepen the meaning of the liturgy in dialogue with our tradition. This is better done in small groups, as I have described, in a safe space with set "rules of the game." And, preachers can, from time to time, point to the relationship between the scripture passages being proclaimed and our liturgical actions. These two modes of reflection will take us very far towards establishing the habit of reflection upon the experience of worship.

In sum, we can and should address our weaknesses in the area of liturgical formation in our church. We can go beyond assuming that liturgical formation is mere explanation or information about the liturgy, to support each other in the life-long work of experiencing worship through signs that fully and transparently embody what they mean. We can also reflect together on our experience of worship and the difference it makes in our daily lives. In these two ways we will continue to grow into the full stature of Christ as limbs of his risen body, living out that great mystery: ". . . Christ and his church" (Eph. 5:32).

Questions for Discussion

1. Make a list of some aspects of your liturgical experience that are very meaningful to you, and another list of aspects that are puzzling, obscure, or baffling. Do the two lists have anything in common or not?

2. Name some aspects of the liturgy in your parish that could be done more fully, without abbreviation.

3. Is there a person in your life whose reflection on the liturgy has helped you grow in appreciation of what we do together in worship? If so, what did they say that was so helpful?

Select Bibliography

Cyril of Jerusalem. *Catechetical Lectures, 19 and 20.* Retrieved February 27, 2022, from https://www.newadvent.org/fathers/3101.htm.

The Didache or Teaching of the Twelve Apostles. Sections 9 and 10. Retrieved February 27, 2022, from http://www.earlychristianwritings.com/didache.html.

Leo the Great. Sermon on the Ascension, 74. Retrieved February 27, 2022, from https://www.newadvent.org/fathers/360374.htm.

McGowan, Andrew B. *Ancient Christian Worship.* Grand Rapids, MI: Baker Publishing, 2014.

Oliver, Juan M. C. *A House of Meanings: Christian Worship in Plain Language.* New York: Church Publishing, 2019.

Otto, Rudolph: *The Idea of the Holy.* Eastford, CT: Martino's Fine Books, 2010.

Rahner, Karl. "The Concept of Mystery in Catholic Theology," *Theological Investigations,* Vol. IV. New York: Herder and Herder, 1973.

Tertullian. *Apology*, 39. Retrieved February 27, 2022, from https://www.newadvent.org/fathers/0301.html.

Wilbricht, Stephen S. *Rehearsing God's Just Kingdom: The Eucharistic Vision of Mark Searle.* Collegeville, MN: The Liturgical Press, 2013.

Wright, N. T. "Being in the Kingdom Today." Retrieved February 27, 2022, from https://ntwrightonline.org/being-in-the-kingdom-today/.